The Black Man in America

1619–1790

Landing African slaves in the American colonies.

The Black Man in America
1619-1790

By Florence and J. B. Jackson

Illustrated with contemporary drawings

Franklin Watts, Inc.
575 Lexington Avenue
New York, N.Y. 10022

for John and Karen

Photographs courtesy of:

The Bettmann Archive; cover, frontis, and pages 10, 14, 22 (bottom), 25, 29, 31, 41, 50, 57, 73
Culver Pictures, Inc.; pages 6, 7, 16, 22 (top), 23, 47, 61, 64, 71
Charles Phelps Cushing; pages 60, 78
The New York Historical Society; page 37
New York Public Library Picture Collection; pages 5, 11, 20, 44, 59, 76
New York Public Library, Schomburg Collection; pages 34, 69

SBN 531 01839-3
Library of Congress Catalog Card Number: 73-101749
Printed in the United States of America

Contents

Introduction   3
Early Jamestown   4
Africans Arrive in Jamestown   9
Indentured Servitude Is Recognized   13
Slavery Takes Root   15
Laws Pave the Way to Slavery   17
Africans and the Demand for Cheap Labor   19
Northerners Enslave Africans   21
Trade Routes to the New World   28
The Journey to the New World   33
A Former Slave Describes Auction Day   36
Training for Plantation Work   40
Slaves Protest Against Slavery   42
Some Whites Oppose Slavery   49
Free Africans in the Colonies   52
A Struggle for Education   55
Black Men Die for American Independence   58
Black People Contribute to American Culture   66
The National Government and Black People   75
Index   81

The Black Man in America

1619–1790

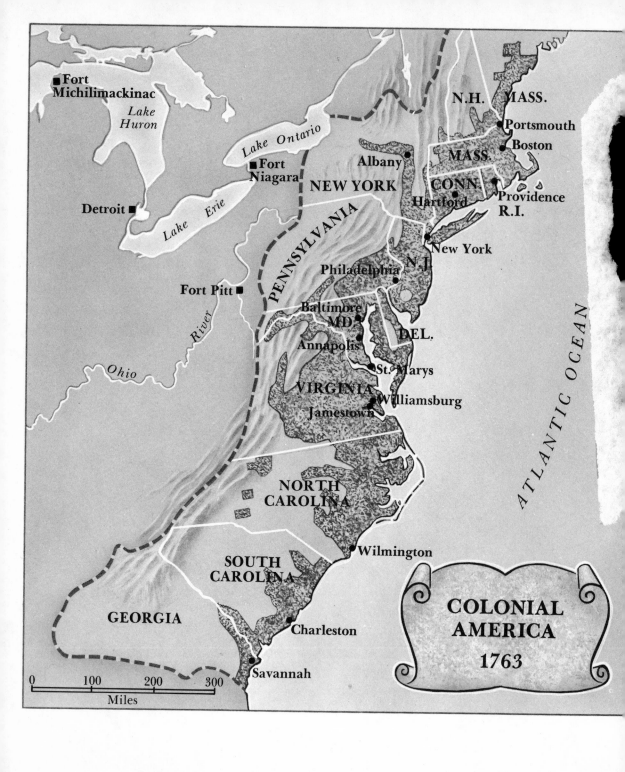

Fort
Michilimackinac

*Lake
Huron*

Lake Ontario

Fort
Niagara

Detroit

Lake Erie

NEW YORK

Albany

N.H.

MASS.

Portsmouth

Boston

MASS.

CONN.

Hartford

Providence
R.I.

New York

PENNSYLVANIA

Philadelphia

N.J.

Fort Pitt

River

Ohio

Baltimore

MD.

Annapolis

DEL.

St. Marys

VIRGINIA

Williamsburg

Jamestown

NORTH
CAROLINA

ATLANTIC OCEAN

Wilmington

SOUTH
CAROLINA

GEORGIA

Charleston

Savannah

0   100   200   300

Miles

**COLONIAL
AMERICA
1763**

Introduction

THE HISTORY of the black man in America began in the year 1619 with the arrival of twenty Africans in the colony at Jamestown, Virginia. The twenty Africans, sold to the colonists in exchange for food, became indentured servants. Since large numbers of white colonists were also indentured servants, black people began life in America on an equal basis with many whites. The white colonists, however, wanting to make large economic profits, played on people's prejudices and ignorance and soon were able to lower the status of the African from servant to slave.

Cries for freedom were made by both blacks and whites before and during the period of the American Revolution. Black people wanted freedom from slavery; white people wanted freedom from England. But when freedom became a reality, it was for whites only.

This book re-creates the history of black people in America from their arrival in the colonies through the time when the United States government was formed. It describes ways in which white colonists lowered the status of blacks in America. Also included in these pages are examples of how black people overcame many obstacles and managed to develop their talents and thus contributed to the culture of early America.

3

Early Jamestown

TOBACCO THRIVED in Jamestown, Virginia. But making a living by growing tobacco meant hard work. The farmer had to plant the seed, cut the plant when it began to ripen, and cure the leaves and pack them for shipment to Europe. A second disadvantage of this crop was that the plants wore out the soil, making it constantly necessary to cultivate the land.

In spite of these difficulties, by 1619 tobacco fields extended outward from the small settlement of Jamestown and along the James River. Naturally, as the number and size of tobacco fields increased, so did the need for labor. To make tobacco cultivation profitable, this labor had to be cheap.

At first, the colonists used Indian workers. They, however, proved unsatisfactory. The Indians had neither the experience nor the skill needed to cultivate large tobacco fields. Another problem arose when the colonists tried to enslave the Indians. Many of them ran away from the farms and returned to their own people. The English settlers, unfamiliar with the land, had little success in recapturing the runaway Indians. Thus, they still needed a source of cheap labor.

Workers would have to be brought into the colonies from abroad. Therefore colonists from Europe were welcomed. Most of the new

Colonists enslave Indians in an attempt to find a cheap supply of labor.

arrivals — orphan boys, convicts, paupers, workingmen, and even some who might be called gentlemen — came as indentured servants. Many were shipped to America, where they were sold by the ship's captain to the highest bidder. Since indentured servitude was already accepted and practiced in England, it was easy to transplant the system to Jamestown. An indenture, or contract, would bind a servant to work for a master for two to seven years, most usually for a period of four years, without wages. The years of service were considered payment for a servant's transportation to America. Some masters took advantage of the indenture and

5

A poor man in Europe might be kidnapped and shipped to the New World as an indentured servant.

made the servants do excessive amounts of work. Indentured servants often worked long hours and received little besides food and clothing for their hard work.

Indentured servants were bound tightly to their masters. If a master died before a contract expired, his servants became part of his estate. A master could sell his indentured servants for profit at any time. In fact, masters considered indentured servants to be property, with the same status as farm animals or household furniture.

Indentured servants often were auctioned off to the highest bidder.

Usually, an indentured servant would become free upon completion of the agreed-upon time in his contract. In addition to freedom, a former servant was sometimes given money, clothing, tools, or seed. These items helped a newly freed servant to start his life in the colonies as a freeman. Now he would be able to work for wages and establish his own home. Later, those who saved enough money could buy land and eventually acquire servants of their own. However, some masters made their servants work beyond the time agreed upon in the contract. For these servants, the end of one contract meant only that another period of service to the master would begin.

For several reasons, white indentured servants, like Indians, also proved unsatisfactory to the colonists. There were not enough white servants to fill the demand for workers. The usually limited period of service made it necessary for a master to keep securing new indentured servants. Masters also had a hard time locating runaways, since the servants could settle among other whites without being detected.

Africans Arrive in Jamestown

ABOUT THE LAST of August, 1619, a Dutch man-of-war sailed into the harbor at Jamestown, Virginia. The name of the ship was not recorded and the reason for its stopping at Jamestown is not definitely known. Where it came from or where it was going did not seem important. On board were twenty Africans taken from a Spanish ship on its way to the West Indies. According to the colonist John Rolfe, the ship's captain offered to sell the twenty Africans for badly needed food. After making the exchange, the mysterious man-of-war sailed out of Jamestown Harbor into the unknowns of history.

It seems likely that during the early period of Jamestown's history Africans became servants in a way similar to whites. After a term of service, they too became freemen — owning property and keeping servants as did other freemen. However, as we shall see later, this arrangement was short-lived for Africans.

During the next fifty years a small number of Africans were brought to Virginia. As the Africans arrived, they were transported to plantations where they worked beside white servants. There seems to have been little concern about physical differences between black and white servants early in the seventeenth century. The two groups worked side by side in the fields, spent their free

In 1619 the first Africans in the American colonies arrived at Jamestown, Virginia.

Jamestown, Virginia, as it appeared in 1622, shortly after the first Africans arrived in the colony.

Virginia colonists imported Africans, first as servants and later as slaves, to work the colony's tobacco industry.

time together, married with one another, and had children. The servants, therefore, practiced some equality of status among themselves.

Indentured Servitude Is Recognized

In 1619 — THE same year the twenty Africans arrived on the Dutch man-of-war — the legislative assembly of the Virginia colony acted on the question of indentured service. The legislative body required that all servants' contracts be recorded and enforced. The recording of contracts made it easy to keep a count of servants in the colony. It also made it more difficult for a servant to run away before his contract expired.

The records had other uses which are of value even today. By examining the Virginia records, one can approximate the number and determine the status of Africans living in the colony during the early period of development. A census made in 1624–25 listed twenty-three Africans living in Virginia. All were referred to as "servants." The Virginia county records from 1632 to 1661 identified Africans as "servants," "Negro servants," or, simply, "Negroes," but not as "slaves." Today many black people consider the term "Negro" as degrading. To them, it refers to the inferior status of the enslaved Africans.

TO BE SOLD, on board the Ship *Bance-Island*, on tuesday the 6th of *May* next, at *Ashley-Ferry*; a choice cargo of about 250 fine healthy

NEGROES, juſt arrived from the Windward & Rice Coaſt.

—The utmoſt care has already been taken, and ſhall be continued, to keep them free from the leaſt danger of being infected with the SMALL-POX, no boat having been on board, and all other communication with people from *Charles-Town* prevented.

Auſtin, Laurens, & Appleby.

N. B. Full one Half of the above Negroes have had the SMALL-POX in their own Country.

An advertisement refers to African slaves only as "negroes." Because the term "negro" was used to mean "slave," many black people today regard the word "Negro" as demeaning.

Slavery Takes Root

BETWEEN 1640 AND 1660, slavery in Virginia fast became an established fact. Historians do not know exactly when Africans became slaves. But it is known that the African population during this period included indentured servants, slaves, and freemen. As time went on, more and more of the servants were threatened with the prospect of becoming permanent slaves.

Both the colonists and the English government recognized and protected white servants' indentures. In contrast, Africans, who were considered foreigners because of their different skin color, lands of origin, and customs, received no protection under English law. Thus it was easy for the colonists to treat the Africans harshly and to change their status from servants to slaves. Legally, slavery was established first by court decisions on specific cases and later by written laws. One method used by the courts to change an African's status from servant to slave is illustrated in the following account of three runaway servants.

Three servants ran away from their master, Hugh Gwyn: Victor, a Dutchman, James Gregory, a Scot, and John Punch, an African. The three men were captured in Maryland and brought back to Virginia to stand trial. The court verdict reached in 1640 stated, "The said three servants shall receive the punishment of whipping

15

Slavery became established in Virginia between 1640 and 1660.

and to have thirty stripes apiece." This much of the punishment was equal for all three. The verdict, however, went on to state that the Dutchman and the Scot should "first serve out their times with their master according to their indentures and one year apiece after the time of their service is expired . . ." and that then they should serve the colony for three years. However, "the third, being a Negro . . . shall serve his said master or his assigns for the time of his natural life." Thus the tone of prejudice and inferior status of the black man was established.

Laws Pave the Way to Slavery

AFTER THE YEAR 1640, most Africans brought to Virginia received no indentures or contracts. Therefore, they could not expect to gain their freedom after a set number of years.

In neighboring Maryland, slavery developed in much the same way as it had in Virginia. In both colonies the first Africans to arrive were servants. During the early colonial period, African servants in Maryland, as in Virginia, gained their freedom upon fulfilling their contracts or after becoming Christians.

More important than the ways in which blacks became free were the ways that they became slaves. Laws were passed that discriminated against blacks and set them apart from white colonists. After the 1660's, both colonies passed laws which made Africans slaves for life. The laws also made it clear that if the mother was a slave, her child would also be a slave. According to these laws, becoming Christians no longer enabled Africans to escape slavery.

SLAVERY AND THE LAW

Virginia,

1662 — Children got by an Englishman upon a Negro Woman, shall be Slaves or Free according to the Condition of the Mother. . . .

1670 — All Servants, not being Christians, imported into this Country by Shipping, shall be Slaves for their Life time, but such as come by Land shall serve, if Boys and Girls, till 30 Years of Age, if Men and Women, 12 Years and no longer.

Maryland,

1692 — Where any Negro or Slave, being in Servitude or bondage, is or shall become Christian, and receive the Sacrament of Baptism, the same shall not, nor ought to be deemed, adjudged, or construed to be a Manumission, or freeing of any such Negro or Slave, or his or her Issue, from their Servitude or Bondage, but not withstanding they shall at all times hereafter be and remain in Servitude and Bondage as they were to the contrary notwithstanding.

1705 — . . . all servants imported and brought into this country by sea or land, who are not Christians in their native country shall be accounted and be slaves, and as such be here bought and sold nowithstanding a conversion to Christianity afterwards.

Africans and the Demand for Cheap Labor

SLAVERY WAS NOT to be limited to one or two colonies for one simple reason — it was profitable. The Carolina settlers, seeing other English colonists profiting from the cheap labor, wanted slaves to cultivate their rich lands. Members of the Royal African Company, a group of English businessmen who transported slaves from Africa to the New World, held claim to the Carolina colony. They were interested in having slaves enter Carolina both for the large profits they could make from the trade and to boost the economic growth of the colony through the use of slave labor. The original settlers were encouraged to import slaves. They were offered twenty acres of free land for every African male slave and ten acres for every African female slave brought into the colony in the first year, or ten acres for males and five acres for females brought into the Carolinas during the first five years. Naturally, such an offer persuaded colonists to import as many Africans as they could possibly afford.

In Georgia, another Southern colony, slavery did not begin until the mid-eighteenth century, and there the story was different. The colony was settled by Englishmen released from prison and sent to start a fresh life in the New World. Therefore, trustees held the land and set up restrictions to govern it. According to the restrictions,

19

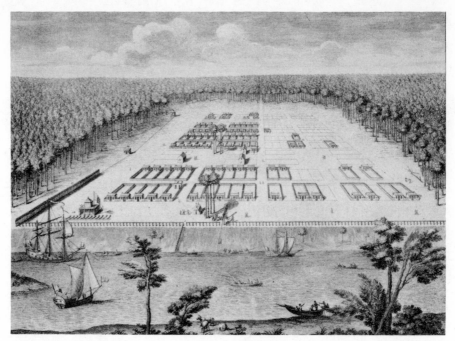

The settlement at Savannah, Georgia, in 1734, shortly before slavery was allowed in the colony.

no African slaves were to be admitted to Georgia. The trustees felt that most of the new settlers would not be able to afford slaves, and even those who might save the necessary funds would be better off rehabilitating themselves. Georgians knew that other colonists owned slaves and were benefiting from their inexpensive labor. Great unrest rose in the colony. Finally in 1741 the restrictions were lifted and Georgia's colonists began hiring slaves from Carolina planters. By 1750 slavery was completely accepted — Georgians were allowed to own slaves.

Northerners Enslave Africans

AFRICANS WERE NOT limited to the South. They were found in New England and in the middle colonies — New York (New Amsterdam until 1664), New Jersey, Pennsylvania, and Delaware — as well. In these colonies, too, Africans were enslaved. Although the emphasis in the middle colonies was on using Africans for trade rather than for labor, there were farms in the region, which, like the Southern plantations, needed cultivation. Therefore, it is not surprising that Northern landowners would seek to introduce slavery — a cheap source of labor — just as the Virginian and Maryland landowners had done earlier. However, the farms in the middle colonies, along the Hudson and Delaware rivers, were much smaller than the Southern plantations, and therefore fewer slaves were needed to work them.

It is not known exactly when the first Africans arrived in New Amsterdam. But colonial records show that as early as 1628, nine years after the twenty Africans arrived in Jamestown, Dutch settlers in New Amsterdam were concerned about the behavior of blacks from Angola. At the time, however, there was no strict set of slave laws or rules established by the Dutch. Africans in New Amsterdam enjoyed some personal rights; few laws restricted their movements. Sometimes freedom was the reward for long or praise-

21

156   From the *New York Gazette,* March 10, 1765

Slaves were found in both the North and the South. This advertisement appeared in the *New York Gazette,* March 10, 1765.

New Amsterdam, about 1660. Hangings took place on the gallows in the background.

The slave market of New York.

worthy services, and freed Africans continued to live in the colony. They bought land in their own names and were allowed to work it for their own profit. Free blacks who were unable to find work sometimes sold themselves into slavery.

The English gained control of New Amsterdam in 1664, and changed the name of the colony to New York. Soon afterward, slave laws similar to those in other colonies were enforced. One law passed in 1665 recognized the enslavement of those Africans who had sold themselves; by 1684 another law recognized slavery as an institution in New York.

As could be expected, Africans in New York were against slavery. When the Africans began to express their discontent, the English began to worry. The unrest among the African slaves and the fear it caused among their masters led to new restrictions of Africans' freedom.

At the session held at the City of New York, October 6, 1694, "For the Better Observation of the Lord's Day," the following law was passed:

No Negro or Indian Servant to meet together above the number of four on the Lord's Day, or any other Day within the City. Nor any Slave to go armed with Gun, Sword, Club, or any Weapon, under penalty of ten lashes at the publick Whipping-post, or to be redeem'd by the Master of Owner at Six Shillings per Head.

In Pennsylvania the colonists were sharply divided on the issue of slavery. Some people were anxious to have African slaves. One person in favor of slavery was William Penn, the English Quaker who founded Pennsylvania as a haven from religious persecution for Quakers. In 1685 Penn expressed the opinion that African slaves were better than white servants since slaves could be kept for life. However, most Quakers and many members of other religions in Pennsylvania felt that slavery was wrong. In 1688, one religious group, the Germantown Mennonites, issued a resolution that stated:

Now, though they are black, we cannot conceive . . . to have them slaves. . . . There is a saying, that we should do to all men like as we will be done ourselves; making no difference of what generation, descent, or colour they are.

It is generally felt that slavery in Pennsylvania was less harsh than that found in other colonies. The slaves often worked alongside their masters on farms or in small stores. But even though the slaves in Pennsylvania may have been treated better than those elsewhere, most Quakers felt that slavery was wrong and should be discontinued. Furthermore, they were not interested in economic gains from the sale and use of human beings.

Other whites — skilled workers, storekeepers, and small farmers — were also against slavery, but for a different reason. The white owners of small businesses or farms had no need for extra laborers.

24

Unlike most Quakers, William Penn, founder of Pennsylvania, believed in keeping African slaves.

They also resented the fact that some men were increasing their wealth by holding large numbers of slaves.

Slavery declined in Pennsylvania. The Quakers not only spoke out against slavery, but they also led a movement to abolish it. Germans living in Pennsylvania joined the Quakers, swelling the size of the anti-slavery group. Large numbers of Dutch and Swedish immigrants who did their own farm work were added to their ranks.

25

Whereas in some other colonies Africans were treated as property, in Pennsylvania, they, like whites, were regarded as human beings. Many Pennsylvanians taught Africans — both slave and free — to read. Others gave them religious instruction. They allowed African slaves to marry and to remain with their families. An import duty required for each African brought into the colony reduced the number of slaves entering Pennsylvania. All of these factors help to explain why slavery did not become a permanent institution in Pennsylvania.

The colonists in neighboring Delaware, although somewhat influenced by what happened in Pennsylvania, tended to follow the policies of the Southern colonies. To increase the slave trade, the Dutch and the English encouraged farmers on the Delaware River to use slaves on their large farms.

In the northernmost colonies of New England, the first African arrivals probably were indentured servants, as they were in Jamestown. It is known that, in 1638, a ship named *Desire* sailed into Boston Harbor. Its cargo included produce and Africans. However, some historians have suggested that the first Africans may have arrived as early as 1624.

It seems strange that slavery was allowed to exist among the freedom-loving Puritans of New England. The Puritans, Englishmen who came to the New World in search of religious freedom, thought nothing of denying personal freedom to black people. Even though Puritan leaders expressed the thought that people who did not believe in their religion should not be allowed to live in the Massachusetts Bay Colony, they readily accepted non-Puritan Africans in order to enslave them. To justify their actions, Puritans claimed a religious belief that Africans were a cursed people who had to be enslaved and exposed to religion.

In 1641, the Puritans issued a now famous document titled, "Liberties of the Massachusetts Colony." It included liberties for men, women, children, strangers, and even animals. Statements relating to slavery contradict one another. One part mentions that there should never be bound slavery in the colony, but another part states that slavery is acceptable under certain conditions. Actually, slavery was allowed if the enslaved people were captured in wars, willingly sold themselves, or were sold to the Puritans. Since most slaves were sold to the colonists, the document gave the Massachusetts colonists legal freedom to hold slaves.

Trade Routes to the New World

EUROPEAN COUNTRIES, such as Spain, Holland, France, Denmark, and England began to acquire islands in the Caribbean in the sixteenth century. To the Europeans, these islands were a source of wealth, not a place to live. The islands had warm climates and rich soil; they were perfect for growing such crops as sugar and tobacco. The Europeans developed large plantations that needed great numbers of laborers to maintain them. To produce the hoped-for profits, this labor had to be cheap.

It was also in the sixteenth century that enslaved Africans were brought to the islands to work on the plantations. As large numbers of Africans began to arrive, they were trained, or "seasoned," for plantation work. There was a growing demand for seasoned slaves to work the plantations on other islands and, later, in the American colonies. Early in the eighteenth century, when prosperity in the Caribbean Islands declined, the Europeans turned most of their attention to the business of exporting slaves. The Europeans developed large trading companies to supply slaves to fill the enormous demands of the Americans.

In time, there was enough business for both European and American slave traders from New England. At first the New England traders, with their smaller ships and lesser amounts of money, had

In the 1500's, African slaves arrived on several Caribbean islands to work European-owned plantations.

a hard time competing with large European trading companies. However, by 1713 the growing demand for slaves created a need for more ships. The New England slave traders could help fill this need and they were more than welcomed.

Because of the sharp increase in trade, the first half of the eighteenth century is often called the golden age of the New England slave trade. Massachusetts led the New England colonies in trading slaves. The colony also played the greatest role in forming what is known as the triangular trade. The triangular trade took its name from the shipping route from New England to the west coast of Africa, to the West Indies, and back to New England. This route formed three sides of a triangle. The ships carried goods, such as rum and fish, from New England to Africa. There the goods were exchanged for Africans. Then the ships continued on the dreaded "middle passage" to the West Indies, where those Africans who survived the crossings were exchanged for molasses. The molasses, taken back to New England distilleries, was made into rum.

Frequently, a ship would stop at the Southern colonies to sell those Africans still remaining on board. Many times, the demands of the Puritan masters brought Africans to New England. Often

The triangular trade route took its name from the shipping route from New England to the west coast of Africa, to the West Indies, and back to New England. The route formed three sides of a triangle.

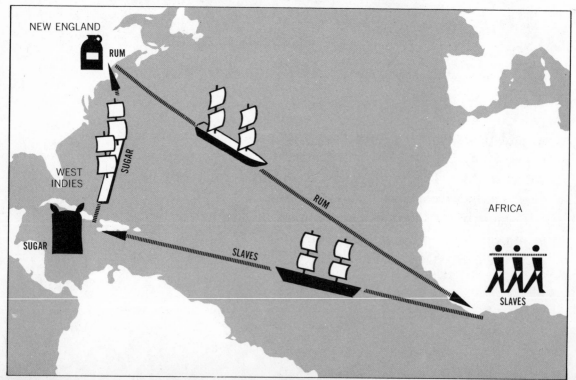

Slaves in the West Indies load sugar on a ship bound for England. This picture appeared in an English children's book. The words with it went:

> The ships to English country go,
> And bear the hardly gotten treasure.
> Oh, that good English men could know.
> How negroes suffer for their pleasure.

only the weaker or less able Africans reached New England, as the West Indian and Southern planters chose the strongest Africans to work their fields. On occasion, New England traders announced the arrival of "lusty strong" or "well-limed" [sic] slaves.

Other New England colonies — Rhode Island, Connecticut, and New Hampshire — also had ships participating in the triangular trade. During the eighteenth century, however, these colonies were not nearly so active in trade as was Massachusetts.

The Journey to the New World

FOR THE SLAVE, life was a series of wretched experiences — from his trip to America to his sale at auction and the life that followed as a slave. Oloudah Equiano, who was renamed Gustavus Vassa, was kidnapped from his family in Africa and placed on board one of the ships that sailed across the "middle passage" to America. He was able eventually to gain freedom from slavery and sail to England, where he later wrote about his experiences.

Vassa described the horror of the "middle passage" in his book, *The Interesting Narrative of the Life of Oloudah Equiano or Gustavus Vassa the African*, as follows:

> At last, when the ship we were in had got in all her cargo, they made ready with many fearful noises, and we were all put under the deck so that we could not see how they managed the vessel. But this disappointment was the least of my sorrow. The stench of the hold while we were on the coast was so intolerably loathsome, that it was dangerous to remain there for any time. . . . The closeness of the place, and the heat of the climate, added to the number in the ship, which was so crowded that each had scarcely room to turn himself, almost suffocated us. This produced copious perspirations, so that the

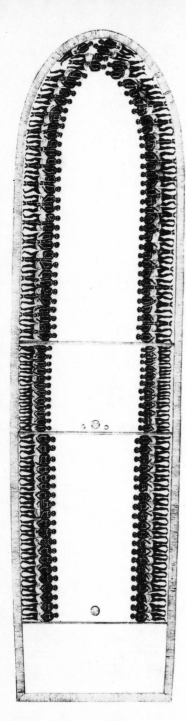 

Slaves packed on ships in inhuman conditions for the voyage to America.

air soon became unfit for respiration, from a variety of loathsome smells, and brought on sickness among the slaves, of which many died. . . . This wretched situation was again aggravated by the galling of the chains, now become insupportable; and the filth of the necessary tubs into which the children often fell, and were almost suffocated. The shrieks of the women, and the groans of the dying, rendered the whole scene of horror almost inconceivable.

A Former Slave Describes Auction Day

A NUMBER OF religious groups as well as some individual colonists believed that slaves should learn to read and write. Interested colonists saw to it that their slaves were taught these skills. In some cases the master or mistress was the instructor; in others, the slaves were sent to small religious schools. Several slaves who obtained freedom later recorded their past experiences. Frequently such accounts revealed the inhuman treatment suffered on auction day. Some of the writings describe how slaves were stripped of their clothing and placed naked upon platforms to be examined by prospective buyers. After this humiliating examination, the auction would begin. Buyers bid for Africans as though they were cattle. Auction day was especially sad for those slaves whose families were broken up. Parents and children often were sold to different masters or traders. The slave sold to a trader would be sold again to some other person. And the sale would probably occur in a distant place, far away from the rest of the slave's family, whom he would probably never see again.

In his book, *Slavery in the United States: A Narrative of the Life and Adventure of Charles Ball, a Black Man*, Charles Ball described his experience and feelings about his separation from his mother, brothers, and sisters after they were sold to different buyers. Ball wrote:

After the horror of the voyage to America, slaves were herded like cattle across land to slave markets for auction.

My mother had several children, my brothers and sisters, and we were all sold on the same day to different purchasers. Our new masters took us away and I never saw my mother, nor any of my brothers or sisters afterwards. This was, I presume, about the year 1785. . . . I learned subsequently, from my father, that my mother was sold to a Georgia trader, who soon after that carried her away from Maryland. Her other children were sold to slavedealers from Carolina, and were also taken away, so that I was left alone in Calvert county, with my father, whose owner lived only a few miles from my new master's residence. My new master took me before him on his horse, and started home; but my poor mother, when she saw me leaving her for the last time, ran after me, took me down from the horse, clasped me in her arms, and wept loudly and bitterly over me. My master seemed to pity her, and endeavoured to soothe her distress by telling her that he would be a good master to me, and that I should not want any thing. She then, still holding me in her arms, walked along the road beside the horse as he moved slowly, and earnestly and imploringly besought my master to buy her and the rest of her children . . . but whilst thus intreating him to save her and her family, the slave driver, who had first bought her, came running in pursuit of her with a raw hide in his hand. When he overtook us he told her he was her master now, and ordered her to give that little Negro to its owner, and come back with him.

My mother then turned to him and cried, "Oh, master, do not take me from my child!" Without making a reply, he gave her two or three heavy blows on the shoulders with his rawhide, snatched me from her arms, handed me to my master, and seizing her by one arm, dragged her back toward the place of sale. My master then quickened the pace of his horse; and as we advanced, the cries of my poor parent became more and more indistinct — at length they died away in the distance. . . . Young as I was, the horrours of that day sank deeply into my heart, and even at the time, though half a century has elapsed, the terrours of the scene return with painful vividness upon my memory.

Following their sale on the auction block, most newly purchased slaves were taken off to plantations by their masters. There they were exposed to a strange way of life which they never could have imagined in their homelands.

Training for Plantation Work

MOST OF THE Africans came from the west coast of Africa and represented many tribal and ethnic groups. Among the slaves were Yorubas, Ibos, Efiks, and Binis from what is now Nigeria. Mandingos and Hausas came from the western Sudan; Ashantis and Fantis from the Gold Coast (now Ghana); Dahomeans from Dahomey; and Senegalese from Senegal. The Africans from these various lands had some things in common, but in many ways they were different from one another. Each group possessed its own highly developed skills that had been influenced by geography and culture. Africans brought a knowledge of agriculture and an understanding of an economy which in some places resembled the plantation system. There were many skilled craftsmen among the slaves — wood-carvers, basket makers, weavers, potters, and iron-workers.

In America, however, the Southern colonists paid little or no attention to the knowledge and skills the Africans brought to the New World. Instead, emphasis was placed on training Africans to do work needed on the plantations. Generally, when the Africans arrived on a plantation, they were assigned in groups to chosen slaves who introduced them to plantation life. The slaves used for this task were called drivers. A driver taught the new arrivals the

Slaves were brought to the colonies mainly to work on plantations. Here, George Washington watches laborers working at his Mount Vernon home.

little English that he knew and trained the newcomers to do plantation work that required little skill. At the end of one year, the master or an overseer of the plantation took over the training and assigned the slaves specific jobs. Unfortunately, the plantation training aimed only at preparing Africans to be slaves. It did not seek to help them further develop their talents.

Slaves Protest Against Slavery

SLAVERY WAS A painful experience. And there was a limit to how much some men could bear. The trip across the "middle passage" horrified the Africans. They were forced to wear chains, to live in stifling quarters, to listen to the agonizing cries of the sick, and to witness the death and burial at sea of mothers, fathers, children, other relatives, and friends. Gustavus Vassa, the former slave who wrote in detail about his trip across the "middle passage," also told of despondent slaves who committed suicide by jumping from the ship into the sea. His description of one such incident follows:

One day when we had a smooth sea and moderate wind, two of my wearied country-men who were chained together (I was near them at the time), preferring death to such a life of misery, somehow made through the nettings and jumped into the sea; immediately another quite dejected fellow, who, on account of his illness, was suffered to be out of irons, also followed their example; and I believe many more would have done the same if they had not been prevented by the ship's crew, who were instantly alarmed.

Then, for those Africans who survived the crossing of the "middle passage," came the numerous hardships in the colonies. Follow-

42

ing the humiliating experience of being sold as a slave at auction, newly arrived Africans faced the extremely harsh working and living conditions on the plantations. They worked long hours with no pay. They were forced to live in miserable housing, survive on inadequate food, and accept punishment for disobeying a seemingly endless list of rules and regulations.

Slaves were not allowed to enjoy even the most basic human rights. They were denied freedom to live as a family without fear of separation. No slave could own a home, or choose a particular type of work. And meetings or gatherings with other black people were prohibited. Because of these unbearable conditions, many Africans preferred to die rather than to live and suffer each day. As a result, there were many suicides among newly arrived slaves. Suicide became a form of protest.

It could be expected that some of those slaves who continued to live under the harsh conditions would rebel. Thus, the colonists became fearful and suspicious. A gathering of slaves might mean that an uprising was being planned. As each rumor of a poisoning in a neighboring county spread, new fears and suspicions grew. Unexplained fires, discoveries of secret meetings among slaves, the sullen looks of slaves when they were punished, all helped to make the slaveholders more nervous.

The colonists reacted to their increasing fears of rebellions by passing laws that restricted meetings and movements among the slaves. By the late 1600's, Virginia already had a set of laws for restricting slaves. These laws, called Black Codes, dictated what was expected of slaves. One law required written permission from the master before a slave could leave the plantation on an errand. Slaves found without a "pass" were immediately returned to the plantation.

When the offenses were more serious, special courts tried the

43

Runaway slaves were hunted and shot down like animals.

cases. These courts consisted of a justice of the peace and two slave owners other than the one involved in the case. The penalties decided upon by the courts varied from whippings to burning at the stake. The punishment for murder was hanging. A slave found guilty of robbing was whipped, placed in a pillory, and had his ears cut off. Another form of punishment for runaways was branding.

By the early eighteenth century both Southern and Northern colonies had Black Codes. Some of these codes kept the slaves from rebelling and seeking their human rights. The Northern codes, however, tended to be less harsh than those in the South.

One example of Southern severity was found in South Carolina.* In that colony any female slave who had run away for the fourth time was severely whipped and branded on the left cheek with the letter R (meaning rogue). As additional punishment, her left ear was cut off.

In all the colonies, in the North as well as in the South, slaves

*In 1712 the Carolina colony split into North Carolina and South Carolina.

44

would run away to seek freedom and to protest against the cruelty of their masters. Those in the South usually headed for the North. Many slaves ran away to avoid punishment for not attending to tasks assigned them. Others ran away to revenge punishment already received. Still others left miserable living conditions. But the greatest force for making slaves run away was the desire for freedom.

Most of the runaways were under the age of thirty and the majority of them were males. Among them were field hands, house servants, and skilled artisans.

The increasing number of runaway slaves resulted in a great economic loss for the masters. The colonists feared that runaway slaves would affect the safety of everyone. They felt that valuable property would be stolen — since runaway slaves needed food and clothing — and that successful runaways would encourage other slaves to do the same.

Faced with the problem of recapturing runaway slaves, some masters began to place descriptions of these slaves in newspapers. Almost every issue of every newspaper published in the colonies contained such advertisements. Descriptions of runaway slaves were also posted in public places in towns and cities. As a result of these efforts, a great deal of time, energy, and money were spent trying to solve the problem of dealing with the runaway slave.

Severe penalties were enforced by the colonists to discourage servants and slaves from running away. In 1643, Virginia issued an order requiring runaway servants to serve an additional amount of time, equal to the period that they were absent from their duties. Second offenders were to be branded with an R. The extreme penalties of branding and disfiguring identified chronic runaways. They also served to frighten slaves who might have thought of running away.

Another method of protesting slavery in the eighteenth century was through a petition for freedom. In one petition written to the governor of Massachusetts Bay in 1773, the status of the slave in the colonies was very effectively explained. "We have no Property! We have no Wives! No Children! We have no City! No Country!"

Slaves constantly revealed their hatred of slavery. As early as 1663, slaves in Virginia held secret meetings to discuss ways of rebelling against their masters.

It is believed that a conspiracy took place in New York City in 1741. Both blacks and whites were involved in what was considered to have been a plan to burn down the city.

A previous uprising in the city in 1712 had left the white citizens fearful that both free and enslaved blacks would again rebel against the whites. In an attempt to guard against another uprising, the colonists enforced more restrictive rules and regulations. There were additional restrictions placed on the movement of black people within the city. Gatherings of more than three black people were not allowed. If more than three blacks were caught talking to one another on the street, they were tied to whipping posts and lashed forty times on their bare backs. Black people resented both the rigid control of freedom and the harsh punishment received by those who were arrested.

During the period between May 11 and August 29, 1741, numerous fires broke out in New York City. In one of the most disastrous fires, the governor's house burned to the ground. As many as four fires occurred in one day. Whites became more frightened and expressed suspicions that black people were setting the fires. Even though it became known that blacks were not responsible for many of the fires, the whites continued to spread rumors. Suspicions turned into accusations, and terror spread throughout the

New York, 1741. Blacks are sentenced following what was believed to have been a plot to burn down the city.

city. Accused persons — both black and white — were seized and thrown into jail. As the fear and terror spread between both races, the city council met to discuss the situation. One member, City Recorder Daniel Horsemanden, said that the fires were caused by enemies within the city. The council reacted by offering a reward or a pardon to anyone who could provide information about the plot. There were rewards of $100 to whites, $45 to free blacks, Indians, or mulattoes, and $20 and freedom to slaves. The desire for either a reward or freedom encouraged both blacks and whites to name people involved in a conspiracy. The accusations started a "witch-hunt" in the city.

Those blacks and whites already arrested feared execution, and some began to offer information about the fires. A white indentured servant, Mary Burton, made a series of charges involving three blacks named Prince, Caesar, and Cuffee and her white master, Hughson. She claimed that the four men planned to burn down the city and kill all whites. Hughson, she claimed, was to set himself up as a king. Caesar would be his governor. Although Mary Burton's accusations seemed ridiculous, the authorities were so caught up in hysteria that they accepted her story. Later, when Mary Burton's claims were investigated, she was found to be lying. By this time, many people had been hurt. One lie had led to another, each of which brought about more arrests and executions.

By the time the panic was over, one hundred and fifty slaves and twenty-five whites had been arrested. Four whites and thirteen slaves had been burned alive, eighteen blacks had been hanged, and seventy others had been shipped out of the colony. It is impossible now to tell whether there really was a slave conspiracy. Some historians believe the "plot" was a conspiracy. Others think that it was a frame-up. The truth may lie somewhere between the two.

Some Whites Oppose Slavery

THESE MANY DIFFERENT means of protest — suicide, petitions, running away, uprisings, conspiracies — brought the evils of slavery to the attention of some whites and caused them to speak out against slavery. Even though antislavery expressions were not widespread during early colonial times, some protest against the slave trade can be traced back to the seventeenth century.

As we have seen, the Germantown Mennonites first spoke out against slavery in 1688. This attack made some individuals think about the injustices reserved for black men. John Woolman, a Quaker living in New Jersey, began in 1743 to speak out against slavery. He was able to convince many New Jersey citizens to accept his views. But although some colonists listened to Woolman, no great stand to oppose slavery was made by any organized group. In the Northern colonies little attention was paid to the problem of slavery. In the South, the enslavement of the black man was becoming more and more accepted.

However, by 1763, antislavery views were being widely expressed for the first time. Such men as Benjamin Rush and Benjamin Franklin worked to free the slaves. James Otis wrote a pamphlet in 1764, titled "Rights of the British Colonies." In the

Colonist James Otis, who believed in freedom for both blacks and whites, wrote a pamphlet entitled "Rights of the British Colonies."

pamphlet Otis stated, "the colonists are by the law of nature free born, as indeed all men are, white or black." Thus, Otis did not overlook the black man's rights to freedom.

Other white men held mixed views toward slavery and the slave trade. Thomas Jefferson, for example, shared the Southern viewpoint that black people were inferior to whites, but he did acknowledge that all men have equal rights. Even though Jefferson himself was a slaveholder, he was not totally in favor of the slave trade. In the original draft of the Declaration of Independence, Jefferson included a paragraph that denounced the slave trade. However, when the document was submitted to the delegates of the Continental Congress, they removed this paragraph. Later, Jefferson explained in his autobiography that the paragraph was omitted because Southerners wanted the slave trade to continue. He did not, however, remove all blame from Northerners, for many of them made considerable profits by transporting slaves. Some historians regard the omission of this paragraph as a serious setback to black people in America.

Free Africans in the Colonies

ALTHOUGH MORE and more African servants in both the South and the North became slaves after 1640, many became freemen. Freedom was achieved in a number of ways. Some slaves were freed by an act of legislation. These acts required that slave owners register the discharge of any slave in the court records. Other slaves gained their freedom through a statement in their masters' last will and testament. Sometimes masters specified in their wills that certain or all of their slaves should be freed. Many times slaves received freedom as a reward for long and praiseworthy service. And more fortunate slaves were able to purchase their freedom and possibly that of other members of their families. This process which enabled slaves to become free legally is called manumission.

One legally freed African was Francis Pryne, who was discharged from servitude in Northampton County, Virginia. The court record of the discharge reads as follows:

> I Mrs. Jane Elkonheade . . . have hereunto sett my hand yt ye aforesd Pryne (a negro) shall bee discharged from all hinderances of servitude (his child) or any (thing) yt doth belong to ye sd Pryne his estate.
>
> Jane Elkonheade

Slaves who worked in towns had more opportunities to save enough money to meet the price they would bring if sold on the market. These slaves were skilled workers. They were blacksmiths, carpenters, tailors, shoemakers, cabinetmakers, painters, plasterers, and seamstresses.

To accumulate the money they needed, town slaves worked nights and Sundays. They hired themselves out to other masters and used their skills on specific jobs until they had saved enough money to buy their freedom. Some masters — those who were more sympathetic or generous — allowed their slaves to buy their freedom in installment payments. Some even lowered the market value of their slaves.

There are accounts of male slaves who worked to purchase their wives and children. At times, wives worked to buy their husbands. Some mothers remained slaves themselves but worked so that their children might become free.

Although there were several ways in which slaves could gain freedom, there were many problems that kept most from becoming free. It was even difficult when a master agreed to let a slave buy his freedom. Usually, several years would pass before a slave could save the money he needed. Sometimes a master would change his mind. In other cases a master died before the slave could purchase himself, and the master's heirs did not recognize the agreement. Slaves who hired themselves out to other masters at times had difficulty collecting fees. There were even instances when a slave was sold before he could save the required money. In such a case the slave had to make a bargain with his new master, who might ask a higher price.

Even though the number of freed slaves grew, the hopes, wishes, and dreams of freedom for many of those still enslaved would not become a reality. Instead their lives were to be filled with demands for hard work without pay, fear of separation from family members, inadequate housing and food, and the frustration of having a status not much above that of farm animals.

By 1790, 32,543 free blacks were living in the Southern states. But 641,691 blacks were still living in slavery. In the North, slavery was gradually disappearing. Of the blacks living in the Middle Atlantic states, about 28 percent, or 14,000, were free. In the New England states, with a total black population of 13,000, about 9,300, or almost three-fourths, of the blacks were free. Vermont and Massachusetts, both in New England, reported that no slaves lived in their areas. Connecticut had the largest number of slaves in New England. By 1790, of 3,700 slaves in New England, 2,600 were living in Connecticut. As a whole, however, the number of slaves continued to decline in New England.

A Struggle for Education

ALTHOUGH LARGE numbers of black people, free and enslaved, were denied opportunities to obtain schooling, we already have seen how many learned to read and write. These talents and others were developed through the help of interested masters and religious groups. Slaves in New England had the best chance of getting some education because the laws in these colonies did not prohibit the teaching of slaves. Fortunately for the slaves, New Englanders had great respect for learning and devoted time to such activities as reading the Bible or almanacs. The almanacs included a calendar, weather predictions, proverbs, agricultural and medical advice, jokes, and a little history. This respect for learning and the use of slaves as clerks in stores and in printing establishments gave slaves in the New England area a better opportunity to learn to read and write.

However, the major force which pushed for the education of black people was the Church. Religious groups, either out of a belief that Africans should be taught how to read the Bible so that they might become "good Christians," or through a genuine desire to educate black people, started classes for them. Even the Puritans, who preached the exclusion of those who did not believe in their religion, taught blacks. The Puritans wanted to fulfill their religious teachings as well as to keep slaves. They, too, wanted to enjoy the economic benefits of slavery. Thus, it was necessary for masters to teach their slaves Puritan beliefs. Since Puritan beliefs were based on the Bible, it made sense for slaveholders to teach their slaves to read the sacred book.

Several Puritan leaders continued to urge slaveholders to give their slaves religious instruction. One such Puritan was Judge Samuel Sewall, who, in 1701, wrote a pamphlet titled "The Selling of Joseph." In the pamphlet, Judge Sewall not only urged religious instruction for slaves but also attacked the practice of making men, the Africans, property.

Another Puritan, Cotton Mather, taught many slaves himself and in 1717 started a school for Indians and Africans. Unfortunately, the school remained open for just a few months. In spite of Puritan wishes to give religious training to the Africans, the continuation of such teaching was eventually discouraged. One important reason for this decline was that membership in the Puritan church opened the way for voting and holding political office. The Puritans were not ready to grant what they considered special privileges to black people.

The Anglicans, another religious group, also made attempts to give slaves some education. In 1705, The Society for the Propagation of the Gospel in Foreign Parts established a school for Africans in New York City. Forty years later, they set up another school in Charleston, South Carolina, and hired two former slaves as teachers. The two teachers, known only as Harry and Andrew, were freed and trained to teach in the school.

Of all the religious groups, the Quakers were most concerned with educating the Africans, especially those who had gained their freedom. Anthony Benezet, a Philadelphia Quaker, established a

Philadelphia Quaker Anthony Benezet worked during much of his lifetime to educate Africans.

school for Africans in 1759 and continued to be involved with the education of Africans until his death in 1784. As a result of his experiences with black children, Benezet wrote that he could "with Truth and Sincerity declare . . . that the notion entertained by some, that the Blacks are inferior to the Whites in their capacities, is vulgar prejudice, founded on the pride of Ignorance of their lordly Masters, who have kept their slaves at such a distance, as to be unable to form a right judgment of them."

Black people who had the means and ability to teach others helped those who were less fortunate than they. One such man was Prince Hall, who was born in Barbados in 1748 and who arrived in Massachusetts when he was seventeen. He became a Methodist minister in Cambridge, Massachusetts, and was very active in Boston's black community. Prince Hall spoke out against slavery, and in 1798 he established in his home a school for black children.

57

Black Men Die for American Independence

MANY COLONISTS who argued for natural, or God-given, rights were concerned over the conditions of the slaves. Anthony Benezet, who had previously spoken out against slavery, described the slaves as being "as free as we are by nature." Americans spoke increasingly about the natural rights of man. Natural rights, they said, belonged to all men. And those colonists who believed in natural rights argued strongly against slavery. As a larger number of colonists began to demand natural rights for themselves, some of them came to realize that their slaves were denied similar rights. Newspapers and pamphlets of the times printed articles which condemned the colonists for keeping slaves while seeking freedom from England for themselves.

Meanwhile the conflict between the colonists and the British grew more intense. The colonists resented the British soldiers sent from England to enforce customs laws. Gangs of colonists did whatever they could to annoy the British soldiers. Name-calling and frequent fighting constantly disturbed the peace. These outbursts irritated both civilians and soldiers. Each group came to distrust the other. Finally, the frequent fights, mutual distrust, and general resentment erupted.

On the night of March 5, 1770, a crowd of angry civilians and a

An advertisement for runaway slave Crispus Attucks, the first man to die during the Boston Massacre, March 5, 1770.

group of British soldiers clashed on King Street in Boston. Five civilians died during the skirmish. The event was later called the Boston Massacre. Many stories were told about the massacre. Some stories described the civilians as a mob carrying sticks and clubs. Others described the civilians as rioters.

Witnesses to the massacre agreed on one fact — Crispus Attucks was the first to die during the Boston Massacre. It is believed that Attucks was a runaway slave who had found work on a whaling ship. Twenty years before the Boston Massacre, a Boston newspaper carried an advertisement for a runaway slave named Attucks. The colonists were not affected by the fact that a black man, whose status as a freeman was questionable, gave his life in the fight for freedom.

In the years following the Boston Massacre, many more colonists refused to accept slavery and joined the antislavery movement. They asked: How can we deny freedom to black people while seeking to gain our own freedom from England?

The name Crispus Attucks appears at the top of the Boston Massacre Monument, built in honor of the massacre's five victims.

More and more black people became involved in the conflict between the colonists and England. Crispus Attucks was not the only black man to give his life for American freedom from England. Blacks participated in several of the first well-known battles of the American Revolution. During the month of April, 1775, black men marched and fought with the colonists at Concord and Lexington. Peter Salem was a black man who took part in both these battles. Salem, who served in a Framingham company of minutemen, became one of the great heroes of the war. It is believed that Salem

Peter Salem, the black man on the left, in the Battle of Bunker Hill during the American Revolution.

shot British Major John Pitcairn on June 17, 1775, when the major, thinking the British had won the battle, had stood up in full view of the colonists.

During the Battle of Bunker Hill on June 17, 1775, other black men fought on the side of the colonists. Along with Peter Salem, another black hero emerged from that battle. His name was Salem Poor. Later, through a petition to Congress dated December 5, 1775, fourteen colonial officers commended Poor for his behavior and ability as a brave and gallant soldier.

The threat of intensified warfare drew closer and closer. The Continental army was formed in June, 1775. Black men were not mentioned in the call for troops even though several had fought previously with the colonists. However, free blacks volunteered their services and some slaves were freed so that they, too, could join the Continental army. In nearly every colony a few black men were enlisted in the militia.

On July 9, 1775, less than a month after the Battle of Bunker Hill, an order given by the new commander of the army stopped the enlistment of black men. The new commander was George Washington, from Virginia. Washington's order, however, did not affect those black men already serving in the colonial army. But within a few months, a movement aimed at removing all black soldiers from the army began. Congressmen and military men met to discuss whether or not to continue using black men in the army. The final decision was to deny all slaves and other black men the opportunity to serve in the colonial army. For further emphasis, Washington issued another order on November 12, 1775, which instructed recruiters not to enlist blacks.

When Washington issued this second order, he did not know that a proclamation on the question of enlisting black men had

62

been issued. On November 7, 1775, five days before, the former governor of Virginia, Lord John Dunmore, issued a proclamation which read in part, ". . . I do hereby further declare all indentured servants, Negroes, or others (Rebels) free, that are able and willing to bear arms, they joining His Majesty's Troops, as soon as may be. . . ." Dunmore, of course, was on the side of the British. His proclamation was an invitation to all slaves to leave their masters and join the British forces. To slaves, the proclamation promised freedom — every slave's dream.

As expected, the proclamation had a grave effect on the colonists. Many feared the effect it would have on the slaves. Hundreds of slaves responded to Dunmore's promise of freedom. And the Virginians, who lost the largest number of slaves, were outraged at the loss of their property. Washington and the Continental Congress were forced to reverse their directives. The change in enlistment orders affected even Washington's actions — on Christmas Day, 1776, two black men, Prince Whipple and Oliver Cromwell, were with him as he crossed the Delaware River.

In 1777, Congress began to set troop quotas for the colonies, and the use of black men gained wide support. After 1777 the recruitment of blacks became widespread north of the Potomac River. Many blacks volunteered, others enlisted, and some substituted for white draftees. A white draftee who did not want to serve in the armed forces was allowed to send someone in his place. As could be expected, the substitute usually was a slave.

Later, there was a proposal to organize an army of blacks in the South. Such an army would give the colonists a manpower advantage over the British. Colonel John Laurens, who for some time prior to this had suggested that black men be enlisted, was chosen to recruit and organize the army. However, Georgian and South

Colonel John Laurens hoped to organize a black army in the South during the American Revolution. His plan was never adopted.

Carolinian leaders, fearing that armed slaves would lead other slaves to rebellion, refused to cooperate. As a result, the proposal was dropped.

In view of the manpower shortage, many recruiters gladly enlisted black men. Black seamen were a common sight in colonial America. Therefore, the recruitment of black men for the Continental navy was natural. One advantage to enlisting black sailors was the experience they brought with them. Blacks had worked on fishing vessels traveling up and down the eastern coast, and on merchant ships or ships of the British navy.

Black civilians who were not soldiers or sailors also aided the American forces. Many were laborers. Some were messengers or guides, and a few were spies. A Virginian slave named James became a well-known spy who served with Major General Lafayette at Williamsburg and made numerous trips to Portsmouth to deliver messages to other American spies. Lafayette commended James for his work as a spy. Lafayette's commendation later prompted the Virginia Assembly to give James his freedom.

Despite the early attempts to block the enlistment of black men, many blacks served in the struggle for American freedom. Of the 300,000 men in the Continental forces, approximately 5,000 were black.

The period of the American Revolution was a turning point in the colonists' thinking about black men and slavery. Many blacks who served during the war were freed. Blacks who had been free before the war were able to improve their conditions. However, the majority of slaves remained in unchanged conditions on the plantations. For these slaves freedom was still an unfulfilled dream.

Black People Contribute to American Culture

IN SPITE OF THE limited educational opportunities for black people during the seventeenth century, many blacks surmounted the barriers. As mentioned earlier, some whites, including Thomas Jefferson, who later became President, questioned the intellectual ability of black people. Jefferson, in his "Notes on the State of Virginia," wrote, ". . . it appears to me, that in memory they are equal to the whites; in reason much inferior. . . ." Although more and more black people demonstrated their intellectual abilities in literature, oratory, teaching, mathematics, and science, Jefferson never really changed his mind. Unfortunately, Jefferson's remarks followed the black man into the twentieth century. However, by the 1770's many well-known whites loudly denied that blacks were intellectually inferior to whites. Benjamin Franklin, president of the first antislavery society in America, said that "blacks were not deficient in natural understanding."

While the debate about the mental ability of black people continued, some blacks went about quietly proving that they could succeed in their intellectual efforts. One such person was Jupiter Hammon. It is believed that Hammon, a slave on Long Island, New York, was the first black author in America. In 1761, his poem "An Evening Thought: Salvation by Christ, with Penitential

Thomas Jefferson, who drafted the Declaration of Independence, and who later became President, believed that black men were intellectually inferior to whites.

Cries" was published on a broadside — a single sheet of paper printed on one side only. Hammon was very much influenced by the renewed interest in the Wesleyan religion and included many acknowledgments of God in his writings.

Of the many poems and prose writings by Hammon, his publication in 1787 of "An Address to the Negroes of the State of New York" is considered the best. In this address, Hammon wrote about the evils of slavery and urged that black people be set free.

It was also in 1787 that Hammon published a poem to the famous black poetess Phillis Wheatley. In his poem, "An Address to Miss Phillis Wheatley," Hammon urged the young woman to reach for perfection in her writing.

Come you, Phillis, now aspire,
And seek the living God,
So step by step thou mayest go higher,
Till perfect in the word.

Phillis Wheatley was the first black woman and the second woman in America to write a book. She had been born in what is now the nation of Senegal on the west coast of Africa, in about 1753. At the age of seven or eight, she was left on a slave block in Boston. A rich Boston merchant, John Wheatley, noticed the small child and, feeling sorry for her, took her home to his wife. The family named the young girl Phillis and she became personal maid to the merchant's wife.

The Wheatleys soon discovered that Phillis was quick and intelligent and was rapidly learning to read and write. Phillis seized every opportunity to read all the books and papers in the Wheatley household.

At the age of fourteen, Phillis wrote her first poem, which was in praise of Harvard University. She went on to write many other poems. In 1773, she visited England and was greatly acclaimed.

General George Washington received a poem that Phillis wrote as a tribute to him. The general thanked her in a letter dated February 28, 1776. Washington wrote, ". . . as a tribute justly due to you, I would have published the poem, had I not been apprehensive that, while I only meant to give the world this new instance of your genius, I might have incurred the imputation of vanity."

Phillis Wheatley died in 1784, at the age of thirty-one. She left many poems behind. Some of the poems, such as "On Imagination," which follows, were published after her death.

68

Phillis Wheatley, brought to America as a slave, became a famous poetess.

Imagination! who can sing thy force?
Or who describe the swiftness of thy course?
Soaring through the air to find the bright abode,
Th' empyreal palace of the thund'ring God,
We on thy pinions can surpass the wind,
And leave the rolling universe behind:
From star to star the mental optics rove,
Measure the skies, and range the realms above.
There is one view we grasp the mighty whole,
Or with new worlds image th' unbounded soul.

69

While Phillis Wheatley was being praised for her writing, a black man in Maryland was also receiving acclaim for his achievements in the fields of science, mathematics, and astronomy. This man was Benjamin Banneker. He became famous for an almanac he published and for helping to plan the city of Washington, D.C. Banneker was born on his grandparents' farm in Maryland on November 9, 1731. After having been taught by his grandmother to read and write, Banneker entered a private country school near his home. He was a good student and did especially well in mathematics.

Banneker's interest in mathematics did not die when he left school. He remained involved in related activities. As a young man, Banneker decided to use his mathematical knowledge to make a clock.

In 1759, Banneker constructed a wooden clock which kept time and struck the hours. Banneker's clock is believed to have been the first clock made in America. This accomplishment made many people aware of his ability and talent. Some people were surprised to discover that the clockmaker was a black man. For several years following his sudden fame, little was heard of Banneker.

Then, about 1772, a mill was erected by a man named George Ellicott. The mechanical devices of the mill fascinated Banneker, who was a neighbor of the Ellicotts. Banneker spent a great deal of time studying the mill. A deep friendship developed between Banneker and George Ellicott, who appreciated Banneker's interest in the mechanics of the mill and his intellectual ability. Ellicott lent Banneker several books on advanced astronomy and some astronomical instruments. Banneker studied the books and mastered their contents. He even discovered mathematical errors in the books. Word soon spread about the mathematical abilities of the

Benjamin Banneker, known first for his outstanding ability in mathematics, later helped to plan the city of Washington, D.C.

black man named Banneker. People began to seek his advice on the movement of heavenly bodies and weather forecasts. The following question, submitted by Banneker to George Ellicott, demonstrates his poetic, as well as mathematical, talent:

> A Cooper and Vintner sat down for a talk,
> Both being so groggy that neither could walk,
> Says Cooper to Vintner, "I'm the first of my trade,
> There's no kind of vessel but what I have made,
> And of any shape, sir, — just what you will,
> And of any size, sir, — from a tun to a gill!"
> "Then," said the Vintner, "you're the man for me —
> Make me a vessel if we can agree.
> The top and the bottom's diameter fine,

To bear that proportion as fifteen to nine;
Thirty-five inches are just what I crave,
No more and no less, in the depth will I have,
Just thirty-nine gallons this vessel must hold, —
Then I will reward you with silver or gold —
Give me your promise, my honest old friend?"
"I'll make it tomorrow, that you may depend!"
So the next day the Cooper, his work to discharge,
Soon made the new vessel, but made it for large;
He took out some staves, which made it too small,
And then cursed the vessel, the Vintner and all.
He beat on his breat — "By the Powers!" he swore,
He never would work at his trade anymore.
Now, my worthy friend, find out, if you can,
The vessel's dimensions, and comfort the man.

While Banneker pursued his mathematical and astronomical work, a young Haitian was on his way to America. The thirst for adventure brought Jean Baptiste Pont DuSable, a black man born in Haiti about 1745, to America. He landed in Louisiana when he was a young man. Afraid that he might be kidnapped and sold into slavery, DuSable decided to travel to the Northwest into free territory. He became friendly with the Indians and from them he learned to trap animals and survive in the forest. DuSable remained with the Indians and lived in one of their villages for a short time. In 1771, he married a Potawatomi Indian girl.

While trapping animals in what we now call the Midwest, DuSable came upon a large lake which had drainage from rivers and a stream at the mouth. He decided that a trading post would thrive if set up near the lake, because trappers could travel on the water-

Dr. Benjamin Rush, physician and abolitionist, informed the Pennsylvania Abolition Society about the work of Dr. James Derham, a black physician.

ways with much less difficulty than they would encounter by land. DuSable's choice of a site for his trading post proved to be a good one and his business prospered. It is believed that DuSable maintained the trading post for about thirty years before selling it. Many years later the city of Chicago was started on the site of DuSable's trading post. Because of this, DuSable became known as the founder of Chicago.

The news of another black man, Dr. James Derham of New Orleans, came to light when the antislavery worker Dr. Benjamin Rush published a brief account of the physician. Dr. Rush introduced Dr. Derham as a brother in science and presented information about the black doctor's work to the Pennsylvania Abolition Society as evidence of his achievements.

In 1762, James Derham had been born into slavery in Philadelphia. Fortunately for Derham, his master, who was a physician, took an interest in the young boy. The master taught Derham to read and write. He also allowed Derham to help prepare some of his medicine. Young Derham displayed interest, knowledge, and ability in the work that he did for his master. When the master died, a British surgeon who knew about Derham's accomplishments as an assistant bought the boy. When the Revolutionary War ended, the surgeon had to return to England. He sold Derham to a Dr. Robert Dove, a physician from New Orleans. Dr. Dove made Derham an assistant and helped the young man gain his freedom. Within a few years, Derham was able to set up his own practice and to accomplish the work which Dr. Benjamin Rush spoke of before the Pennsylvania Abolition Society.

In spite of the outstanding achievements of brave and accomplished blacks, slavery and inhumanity were not yet to die. By the time that the government of new America was formed, the term "American" still did not apply to all that nation's people.

The National Government and Black People

As we have seen, American leaders debated the issue of enlisting black men in the Continental armies. After the Revolutionary War, black people were again a topic for debate. By 1784, the debate in Congress involved the introduction of slavery in the Northwest Territory.

As a result of large numbers of Americans moving westward, many questions about the settlement of the Northwest had to be answered. One question was in regard to slavery. Should slavery be allowed in the Northwest Territory? This question was voted upon in Congress at three different times between 1784 and 1787. Those members who favored prohibiting slavery in the Northwest Territory won in the final vote. As a result of the vote, a law known as the Northwest Ordinance was passed in 1787. Among the many parts of the ordinance, or law, was the statement, "There shall be neither slavery nor involuntary servitude in the said territory. . . ." The ordinance was the first and most positive action taken by the national government to stop the expansion of slavery following the Revolutionary War.

Even though the national government passed laws, such as the Northwest Ordinance, it was obvious that the government could not solve all of the problems relating to slavery. During the winter

of representatives shall nominate two persons qualified as aforesaid, for each vacancy, and return their names to Congress; one of whom Congress shall appoint and commission for the residue of the term; and every five years, four months at least before the expiration of the time of service of the members of council, the said house shall nominate ten persons qualified as aforesaid, and return their names to Congress, five of whom Congress shall appoint and commission to serve as members of the council five years, unless sooner removed. And the governor, legislative council, and house of representatives, shall have authority to make laws in all cases for the good government of the district, not repugnant to the principles and articles in this ordinance established and declared. And all bills having passed by a majority in the house, and by a majority in the council, shall be referred to the governor for his assent; but no bill or legislative act whatever, shall be of any force without his assent. The governor shall have power to convene, prorogue and dissolve the general assembly, when in his opinion it shall be expedient.

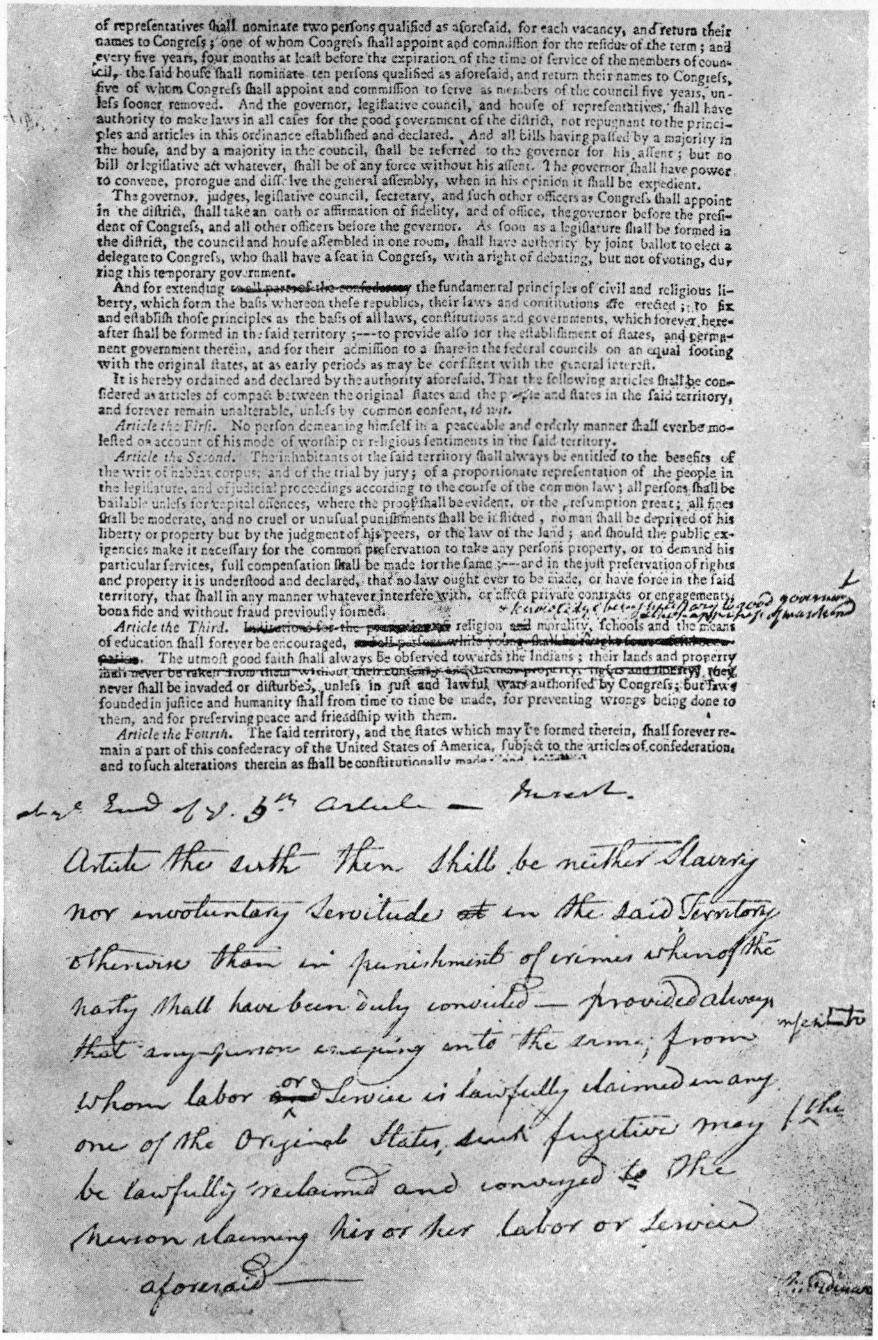

The governor, judges, legislative council, secretary, and such other officers as Congress shall appoint in the district, shall take an oath or affirmation of fidelity, and of office, the governor before the president of Congress, and all other officers before the governor. As soon as a legislature shall be formed in the district, the council and house assembled in one room, shall have authority by joint ballot to elect a delegate to Congress, who shall have a seat in Congress, with a right of debating, but not of voting, during this temporary government.

And for extending to all parts of the confederacy the fundamental principles of civil and religious liberty, which form the basis whereon these republics, their laws and constitutions are erected; to fix and establish those principles as the basis of all laws, constitutions and governments, which forever hereafter shall be formed in the said territory;—to provide also for the establishment of states, and permanent government therein, and for their admission to a share in the federal councils on an equal footing with the original states, at as early periods as may be consistent with the general interest.

It is hereby ordained and declared by the authority aforesaid, That the following articles shall be considered as articles of compact between the original states and the people and states in the said territory, and forever remain unalterable, unless by common consent, to wit.

Article the First. No person demeaning himself in a peaceable and orderly manner shall ever be molested on account of his mode of worship or religious sentiments in the said territory.

Article the Second. The inhabitants of the said territory shall always be entitled to the benefits of the writ of habeas corpus; and of the trial by jury; of a proportionate representation of the people in the legislature, and of judicial proceedings according to the course of the common law; all persons shall be bailable unless for capital offences, where the proof shall be evident, or the presumption great; all fines shall be moderate, and no cruel or unusual punishments shall be inflicted; no man shall be deprived of his liberty or property but by the judgment of his peers, or the law of the land; and should the public exigencies make it necessary for the common preservation to take any persons property, or to demand his particular services, full compensation shall be made for the same;—and in the just preservation of rights and property it is understood and declared, that no law ought ever to be made, or have force in the said territory, that shall in any manner whatever interfere with, or affect private contracts or engagements, bona fide and without fraud previously formed.

Article the Third. Religion and morality, schools and the means of education shall forever be encouraged. The utmost good faith shall always be observed towards the Indians; their lands and property never shall be invaded or disturbed, unless in just and lawful war authorised by Congress; but laws founded in justice and humanity shall from time to time be made, for preventing wrongs being done to them, and for preserving peace and friendship with them.

Article the Fourth. The said territory, and the states which may be formed therein, shall forever remain a part of this confederacy of the United States of America, subject to the articles of confederation, and to such alterations therein as shall be constitutionally made.

[handwritten at bottom]

At the end of the 5th article — insert.

Article the sixth. There shall be neither Slavery nor involuntary Servitude in the said Territory otherwise than in punishment of crimes whereof the party shall have been duly convicted — provided always that any person escaping into the same, from whom labor or Service is lawfully claimed in any one of the Original States, such fugitive may be lawfully reclaimed and conveyed to the person claiming his or her labor or Service aforesaid

The Northwest Ordinance of 1787 contained a statement against slavery in the Northwest Territory.

of 1786–87, a group of Massachusetts farmers, who were over-burdened with debt, armed themselves and rebelled under the leadership of Daniel Shays. As there was no United States army to put down the rebellion, the Massachusetts militia was called upon to establish order. This lack of a national army and the inability of the central government to raise revenue taxes emphasized its weakness. Americans were sure now that a strong national government was necessary. To improve the situation, Northern and Southern delegates were called together to frame a new constitution. This constitution would give the national government more power and at the same time represent the American people.

From May to September, 1787, the delegates to the Constitutional Convention met in Philadelphia. Before long, the fifty-five delegates had to discuss a major question about representation. How should the states be represented in the new government? Should slaves be counted for representation?

Most of the Northern delegates said that Southerners considered their slaves as property. Northerners feared that the South would have too much voting power if slaves were counted as part of the population. Elbridge Gerry of Massachusetts, a future Vice-President of the United States, said, "Blacks are property, and are used to the southward as horses and cattle. . . ." Gerry expressed his belief that if the large numbers of slaves in the South could have representation, then Northerners should be allowed to have their cattle counted for representation also. But as the debate continued, the delegates from Georgia and South Carolina demanded that blacks be counted equally with whites. It did not seem to matter to the delegates that slaves could not own property, and therefore, could not vote in most states.

After many long debates on the question of representation, the

77

The issue of slavery was discussed at the Constitutional Convention held at Independence Hall in Philadelphia, in 1787.

Northerners finally agreed to have slaves counted for representation and taxes. However, in the count, every five slaves would be equal to three free white citizens. In return, the Southerners accepted a ban on the importation of slaves, beginning in the year 1808 — twenty years after the convention. The agreement between the Northern and the Southern delegates became known as the three-fifths compromise.

For black people, the formation of a new government and the framing of a new constitution gave little hope that one day slavery would end. Slaves continued to live under the same conditions as they had before the Revolutionary War. Even though both black and white men fought for freedom, the slaves did not share in the freedom gained by the success of the war. The small number of slaves who obtained their freedom by bravely serving in the armies was not large enough to raise the hope for freedom among the great number of black people still enslaved. The three-fifths compromise kept the black man unequal in status to the white man.

The achievements and contributions of free black people were looked upon as individual abilities and not as representative of the abilities of black people as a group. Prejudice and ignorance fed the institution of slavery and allowed it to thrive in the newly freed America.

Index

Abolition. *See* Antislavery movement
Africans, 9, 15, 17, 19, 21, 22, 28, 30-31, 40-41
  arrival in colonies of, 9
  skills and crafts of, 40-41
  See also Blacks
Anglicans, 56
Antislavery movement, 25, 49-51
Armed forces. *See* Continental army, Continental navy
Attucks, Crispus, 59
Auctions, slave, 36
  described by Charles Ball, 38-39

Ball, Charles, 36
  quoted, 38-39
Banneker, Benjamin, 70-71, 72
  quoted, 71-72
Benezet, Anthony, 56-57, 58
Bible, 55, 56

Black Codes, 43, 44
Blacks
  in British army, 63
  in colonial forces, 62-65
  population of (in 1790), 53-54
  skills of, 53
  status at end of Revolutionary War, 79
Boston Massacre, 59
British, 23, 58-59, 63
Bunker Hill, Battle of, 62

Carolina, 19, 44*n*
Children. *See* Slavery
Christianity, 17, 18, 55
Congress, U.S., 75
Connecticut, 31, 54
Constitutional Convention, 77
Conspiracy, 46-48
  See also Rebellion
Continental army, 62, 63

Continental Congress, 51, 63
Continental navy, 64
Cromwell, Oliver, 63

Declaration of Independence, 51
Delaware, 21, 61
Derham, James, 73-74
Desire, 26
Dunmore, Lord John, 63
DuSable, Jean Baptiste Pont, 72-73

Education, 26, 36, 55-57, 66
English. *See* British
Equiano, Oloudah. *See* Vassa, Gustavus

Family life of slaves, 36, 42, 43, 53
Franklin, Benjamin, 49, 66
Freedom, 8, 52, 53, 79
Freemen, 9, 52-54

Georgia, 19-20
Gerry, Elbridge, 77

Hall, Prince, 57
Hammon, Jupiter, 66-67
   quoted, 68

Indenture, 5-6
   See also Servants and servitude
Indians, 4

Jamestown, Virginia, 4, 9
Jefferson, Thomas, 51, 66

Labor, 4, 19-20, 28
Lafayette, Major General, 65
Laurens, John, 63-64
Law and legal decisions, 13, 15, 17, 18, 43-44
   in New York, 23-24
   1640 court verdict, 15-16
   See also Black Codes
"Liberties of the Massachusetts Colony," 27

Manumission, 52
Maryland, 17, 18
Massachusetts, 26, 29-30, 54
Mather, Cotton, 56
Mennonites, 24, 49
"Middle passage," 33, 35, 42
Molasses, 30

Natural rights, 58
"Negro," as a term, 13
New Amsterdam. *See* New York
New England, 21, 26, 54, 55
   slave trade in, 28-31
New Hampshire, 31
New Jersey, 21
Newspapers, 45, 58
New York, 21, 23, 46
Northwest Ordinance, 75
Northwest Territory, 75

Otis, James, 41, 51

Penn, William, 24

Pennsylvania, 21, 24, 25-26
Petition for freedom, 46
Pitcairn, John, 62
Plantations, 40-41
Poor, Salem, 62
Pryne, Francis, 52
Puritans, 26, 27, 55-56

Quakers, 24, 25

Rebellion, 43, 46, 77
Revolution, American, 58, 59, 61, 65
Rhode Island, 31
"Rights of the British Colonies," 49, 51
Rolfe, John, 9
Royal African Company, 19
Runaways
    black, 44-45
    Indian, 4
    penalties for, 45
    white, 8

Salem, Peter, 61
"Selling of Joseph, The" 56
Servants and servitude, 5-6, 8, 13

records of, 13
Sewall, Samuel, 56
Shays, Daniel, 77
Ships. *See* Slave ships
Slavery, 15, 17, 75
    conditions under, 43
    status of children under, 17
Slave ships, 33, 35
South Carolina, 44
Suicide, 42, 43

Tobacco, 4, 28
Triangular trade, 30-31

Vassa, Gustavus, 33, 42
    quoted, 33, 35
Vermont, 54
Virginia, 9, 13, 18, 43, 63
    census of 1624-25, 13
    See also Jamestown, Virginia

Washington, George, 62, 63, 68
Wheatley, Phillis, 67, 68, 70
    quoted, 69
Whipple, Prince, 63
Woolman, John, 49

83

ABOUT THE AUTHORS

Mr. and Mrs. J. B. Jackson are natives of New York City. Both received a bachelor's degree — he a B.A. and she a B.S. — from New York University. Mr. Jackson received his M.S. from Yeshiva University; Mrs. Jackson's was from the College of the City of New York.

Before going into education, Mr. Jackson was a flying instructor, and for many years he served with the Federal Aviation Agency. While awaiting appointment as an assistant principal in a New York City junior high school, he is teaching social studies in a city high school.

Mrs. Jackson was a classroom teacher for several years and then a teachers' consultant. Presently she is developing elementary curriculum at the Bureau of Social Studies for the New York City Board of Education.

The Jacksons live with their two children, Karen and John, Jr., in New York City.